IKWE

IKWE

Honouring Women, Life Givers, and Water Protectors

An Indigenous Art Colouring Book

by

Jackie Traverse

Errata — IKWE

Please note an error in the Foreword. Heather Bourget is a student in Indigenous Studies. She is not an Indigenous student. Fernwood takes full responsibility for this error and apologizes to Heather, Jackie Traverse and all readers.

Foreword

IKWE is the second colouring book created by Anishinaabe artist and activist Jacqueline (Jackie) Traverse of Lake St. Martin First Nation. Jackie was born in Winnipeg, where she currently resides and continues to create in her art studio, Creative Native Sanctuary of Inspired Self-Expression. She is a graduate of the University of Manitoba's Fine Arts Program and founder of IKWE Safe Rides for Women and Rock the Vote Winnipeg, as well as being involved in numerous community-based outreach programs and school-based activities. She is a vibrant, passionate, and kind-hearted woman committed to her own healing and growing journey while loving and mentoring others along the way. I am humbled and honoured to call her my friend.

As an accomplished multidisciplinary artist who works in video, mixed media, and sculpture, Jackie's passion exudes from her painting and drawings. Jackie's art has grounded her in her Anishinaabe roots and has been a source of her own inner healing and empowerment. The arts have always been a venue for non-violent activism, resistance, and holding a mirror to society's atrocities, and Jackie uses her craft mightily with courage and strength. Her beautiful and powerful works convey the strength, beauty, tenacity, and resilience of Indigenous Peoples and women in particular. Jackie's works are featured internationally in Kathmandu, Nepal, New York, throughout North America, and Europe.

Like Sacred Feminine, IKWE serves once again to educate, inspire, empower, enlighten, and heal those of all ages who embark on this creative colouring journey. Her work encompasses the essence of the sacred gift that lies within each woman and seeks to connect them on an emotional, physical, and spiritual level. Each image carries deep meaning and purpose. Jackie explains the representations of each and defines its symbols. The teachings that lie within serve to empower and act as a healing salve to wounded souls and a guiding light to serenity, wisdom, and joy, all while celebrating the beauty of timeless lessons. The intricate details of her work reflect the mindful intentions of her heart. They convey messages that whisper to the soul. Enjoy the journey this process takes you on. Internalize the invaluable knowledge. Experience the beauty you create while calming your spirit and enriching your soul. And share the gift with others.

Heather Bourget
Indigenous Student,
Urban and Inner City Studies and Conflict Resolution Studies,
University of Winnipeg

Dedication

This book is dedicated to my father, Joseph Fabian. He encouraged me with my drawing since I was a little girl, enrolled me in art classes at the Winnipeg Art Gallery when I was eight, and always ensured that I had art supplies. Without my father's encouragement and support, I may have never become the woman I am today. I love you, Dad. Thank you for all that you did for me.

Your daughter,
Jackie

Mother Earth

Cedar Bath

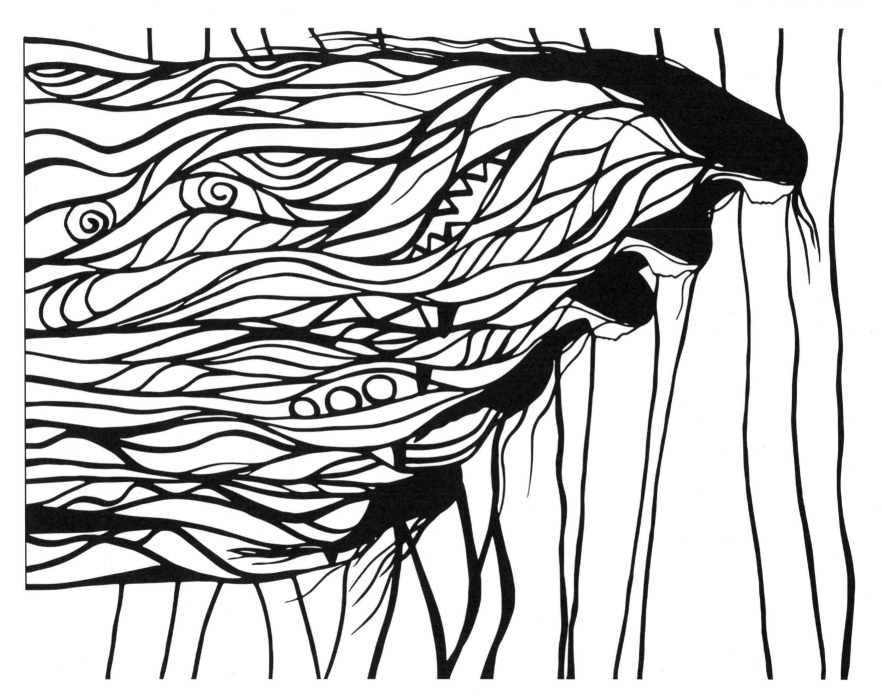

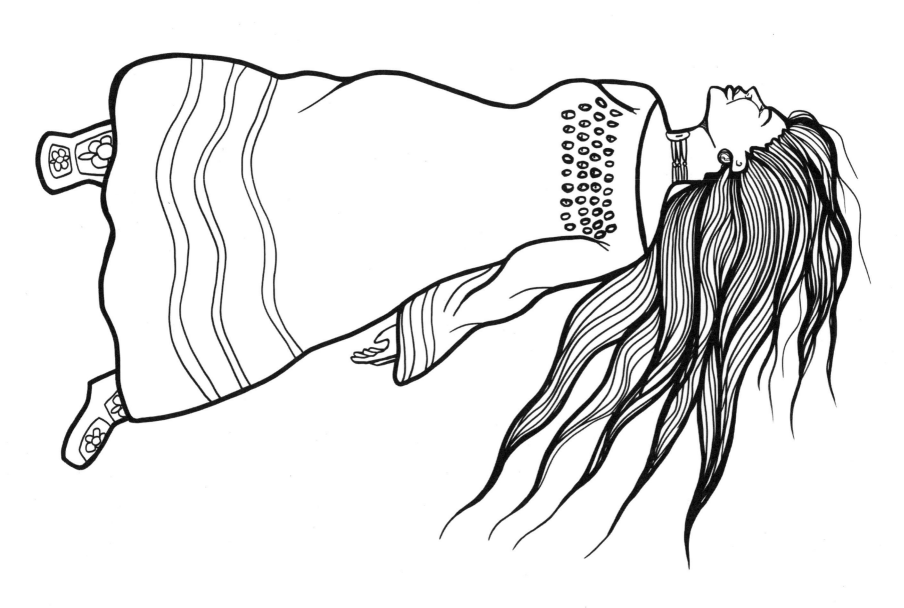

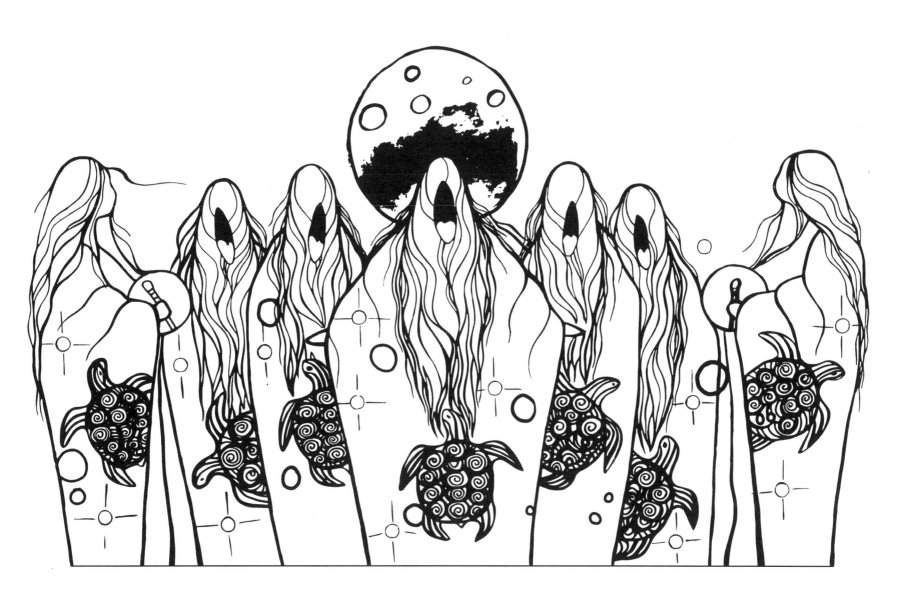

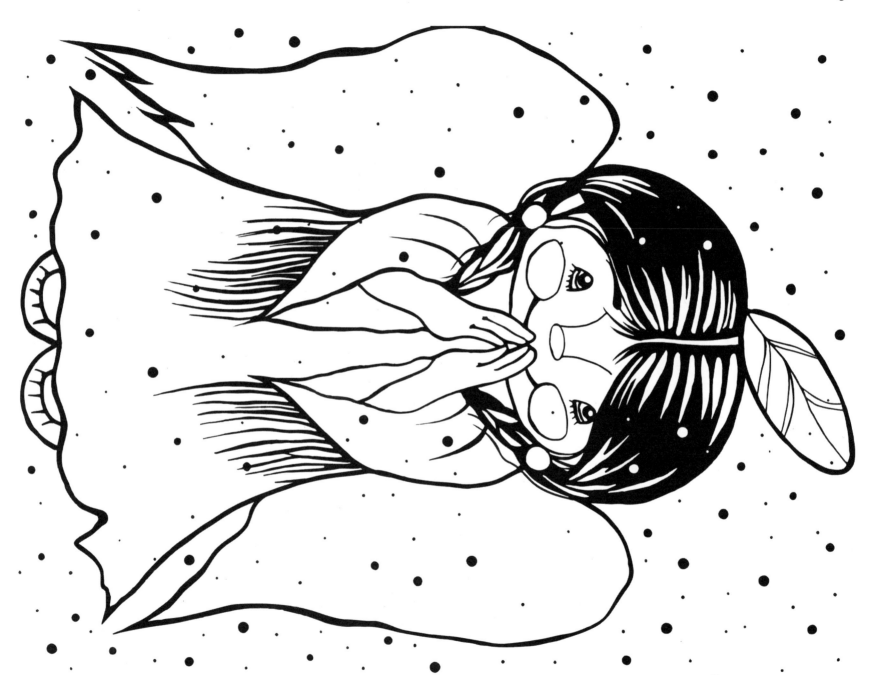

Sky Woman

Strawberry Medicine

Thunderbird Ikwe

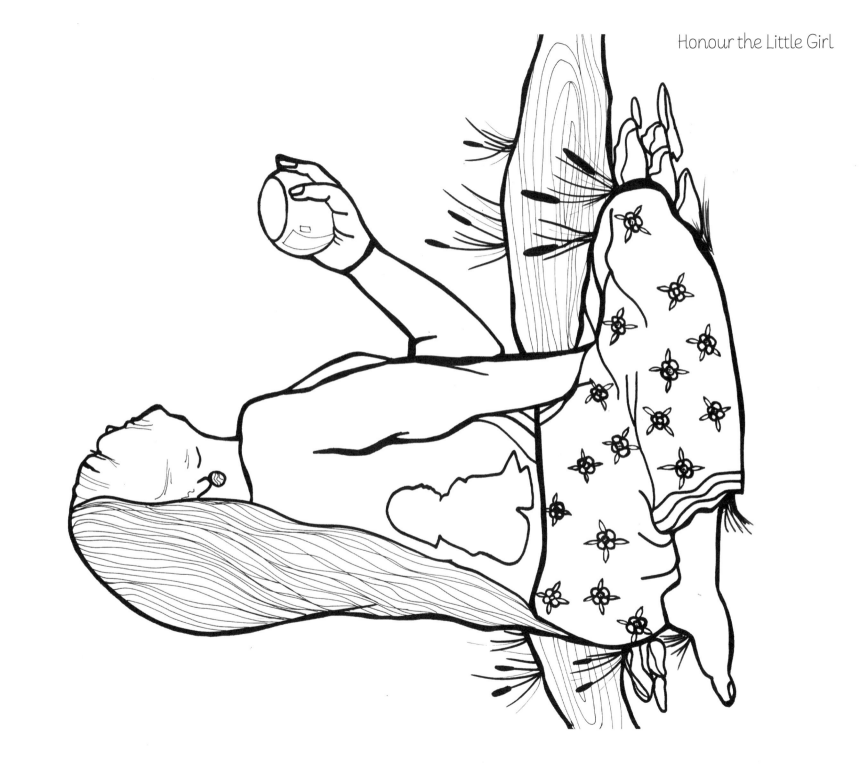

Memengwa Ikwe

Mother and Child Turtle Clan

Mother Earth

We are all children of the Earth, and everything we need to be nurtured and happy in this life comes from our mother – our own mothers and our Mother Earth. Here the mother is cloaked in Ojibwe florals, which bring beauty to our eyes.

Miikiinaak Mother and Daughter

This mother has just finished feeding her baby. The mother provides all the nutrients the baby needs to grow and thrive from her breast. It's the most sacred bond a mother and child could have, besides being housed in Mama's womb for nine months.

Bear Woman

Walk with courage in everything you do. Taking the first step in achieving your goals takes a lot of courage. It's easier to sit by and let things unfold, but if you want something, you have to walk in courage to get it.

Between Two Worlds

Here Eagle is carrying the cloth ties – the prayers of the people – from the Sundance ceremony to Creator; he is between two worlds: the living world and the spirit world.

Cedar Bath

In the Cedar Bath Ceremony, the participant lies on a table and is covered with a sheet. The traditional healer soaks cloths in cedar tea and places them over the participant's eyes and throat and on the crown of the head. Then cedar-soaked cloths are pulled over the participant's body four times. The healer smokes their pipe or sings a song, sometimes also fanning the participant with an eagle fan. Afterwards, the healer and participant share if they saw anything in the ceremony that could help them in their healing.

Cherish One Another

This is me, my three daughters, and my granddaughter Lily: three generations of women in my family. We must cherish women in this lifetime so that our grandchildren will feel that love.

Courageous

My life has been defined by courage. When I was in art school, I was told by three professors that I'd probably never graduate. Not only did I graduate, but I graduated with a 4.0 grade point average. I have the courage to do what I want. Having courage to pursue what you want means not taking "no" for an answer – especially not from yourself.

Dance to the Beat of Your Own Drum

Women are able to dance through their lives without fear and know in their bones what respect is. My hope for women all across Turtle Island is to feel safe and good in their own skin.

She Leads with Love

Woman embodies love; she loves her children, her family, her community, her people. She loves all living creation.

Harvesting the Hair of Mother Earth

The women are harvesting sweetgrass, the hair of Mother Earth, for cleansing and purity. When you take, you must offer back tobacco.

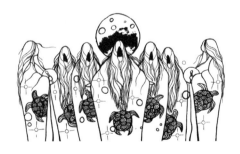

Full Moon Ceremony

The Full Moon Ceremony is a woman's ceremony. We honour Grandmother Moon and sing to her every full moon. We do the ceremony 13 times a year because there are 13 full moons each year. The turtle is woman's teacher. Its back has 13 full moons and 28 markings, which represent women's monthly cycles.

Little Angel

Every Christmas when I was growing up, I would notice that there were no angels who looked like me. They all had blonde hair and blue eyes. That made me feel left out. So I created my own series of Christmas cards and I put my people in there because I know children need to see themselves in a positive way.

Grandmother and Grandfather Teaching

Grandmother and Grandfather are teaching the children about medicine and the smudge inside the turtle petroform at Bannock Point in Manitoba. Out of the smudge bowl come past Grandmothers and Grandfathers because when we pray, our ancestors are always with us. The Grandfather awaits his turn to sing a song while the Grandmother speaks to the children.

Golden Eagle Woman

Golden Eagle Woman is a spirit name that I was asked to paint. The connection to your spirit name is powerful. Many Indigenous people draw strength from their spirit name or clan.

Nokomis Gives a Spirit Name

The animals are coming to Grandmother in a vision of what the child's spirit name will be.

Ojibwe Florals

Some flowers are medicinal, but flowers are mostly here to be beautiful.

On the Wings of Love

My little brother was taken from my mom when he was a month old and adopted by a single white man in Pennsylvania. I've only seen my brother once, and I pray that he had love and inner strength. Here is an eagle transforming, coming out of the sky and giving strength to the little boy.

Prayers for the Water

This angel has come down to pray for the water. Women are the water keepers and the water protectors, a gift that they have had since the beginning of time. We carry our babies in water, and water gives life to everything.

Rainbow Warrior Society

The rainbow is also a clan. Here, these women have the four medicines: tobacco, sweetgrass, sage, and cedar.

Prayers for Turtle Island

Together, we, men and women, are stronger. We should live in a good way and pray for our home, community, children, Elders, and loved ones.

Sky Woman

Sky woman is part of the Creation Story. She lived in the sky world with sky beings, but one day she fell from the sky. The otter and beaver helped her get up, placing her on the back of a turtle, which then became Turtle Island.

Song of the Butterfly

I love butterflies. Sadly, they are the symbol the missing and murdered Indigenous women, but there is also a positive side to their symbolism: metamorphosis. Here, women are singing the song of the butterfly and are happy to transform from one stage to the next, from adolescents to women.

Strawberry Medicine

The strawberry is the medicine of the heart. It is medicine that helps us show each other unconditional love, just as we treated each other before colonization. Love does not judge, it does not bargain, and it does not discriminate: it simply accepts.

Thunderbird Ikwe

Thunderbird woman is bringing rain and spitting out lightning, replenishing the Earth and cleansing all life.

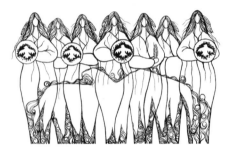

Thunderbird Women

Seven women gave me my name: The Sound of the Thunderbird Approaching. Knowing what my name means has given me so much strength. The four thunderbirds represent the Thunderbird Clan.

Water Protectors

I had the privilege of going to Standing Rock twice. The strength and power that came from the women there inspired this book. To be a woman is to be a life giver and water protector. Even if you never have children, you have that sense and the duty to honour and protect the water. The water is within you.

Wolf Girl

To know your clan and spirit name as a young person is a blessing. It means knowing your protector – the guide who will walk you through life.

Women's Council

In my family, the women are matriarchs. They call the shots. For generations, women made the decisions, meeting in councils and with Elders, and seeking fairness and equality for everyone in the family. Colonization tried to take that power away from the women, but we're reclaiming it.

Honour the Little Girl

This Elder is finding a place where she can forgive, love, and honour the inner child who had a hard time in residential school. She wants to enjoy the rest of her days free of guilt and bad feelings.

Little Eagle Spreads Her Wings

This painting comes from when I was teaching children in an art program that also had dance lessons. I saw the children learning how to dance. They're shy and clumsy, unsure of what to do. But five or six years later, they become champion dancers. This little girl is spreading her wings and taking that chance to learn, to be embarrassed, yet to pursue what her ancestors have always done.

Memengwa Ikwe

Memengwa Ikwe is Butterfly Woman. Butterfly is a symbol for our missing and murdered Indigenous women. She looks like she's in her own thoughts – maybe she's praying for justice, maybe she's praying for the families. That's open to interpretation.

Mother and Child Turtle Clan

Both the mother and her baby belong to the Turtle Clan. The baby is enjoying her mother's embrace. Her mind is filled with the teachings of the turtle, and she yearns to know where she comes from.

Walk with Courage

It can be difficult to be a woman, especially in Canada. You need to draw on the inner strength that's within you, call on your clan, your ancestors, and your grandfathers and grandmothers for the strength to walk in this world every day.

Seven Teachings – Love

Love brings peace. We must love ourselves unconditionally before we can love others, and we should share our love with children and all those who need it. The eagle carries all of the teachings, and at the heart of all of the teachings is love. In all you do, lead with love.

Seven Teachings – Respect

The bison represents respect. The bison gives every part of itself to sustain us humans because it respects the need to keep the world in balance. In turn, we should show respect to Mother Earth and all living creatures, never taking more than we need.

Seven Teachings – Courage

We must have fearless, principled hearts, and stand up to our challenges and fears with integrity, even when we don't know what will happen next. We must do this for our communities, our families, and ourselves. The bear, especially the mother bear, represents strength because she protects her young at all costs.

Seven Teachings – Honesty

Be true to yourself and with others. Live as you were meant to live. The footsteps are those of Sabé, a being that walks tall among humans and sees us for who we truly are. We must also walk tall and accept ourselves for who we are.

Seven Teachings – Humility

Living in humility means understanding that you are part of creation, something bigger than yourself, just as the wolf is part of its pack. It means being selfless and generous, celebrating the achievements of others, and being in balance with all living creatures. The Anishinaabeg learned a lot by watching the wolves. This is why we tend to our Elders and our children first.

Seven Teachings – Wisdom

Wisdom means using the gifts within us to survive and thrive, just like the beaver uses its wisdom to build a home and care for its family. Watch and listen carefully to learn from those around you.

Seven Teachings – Truth

The turtle is an old creature who helped create Turtle Island when Sky Woman landed on its back. The turtle has 13 moons on its back; each one represents a cycle of women's moontime. The turtle is deliberate, slow, stable, patient, and attentive to the smallest details; these are the characteristics of those who know and speak the truth. We should learn patience from the turtle, and we must speak our truth.

Jackie Traverse

Jackie Traverse is Anishinaabe. She graduated from the School of Fine Arts at the University of Manitoba in 2009. A multidisciplinary artist, Jackie works in many mediums, including painting in oils and acrylics to mixed media, sculpture and stop-motion animation.

Jackie's work is women-centred. Her paintings, drawings, documentaries, and sculptures speak to the realities of being an Indigenous woman. She created Butterfly, a stop-motion animation on missing and murdered women and girls in Canada, another on the Sixties Scoop, entitled Two Scoops, and Empty, a tribute to her estranged mother.

The injustices faced by Indigenous Peoples are integral to Jackie's art, leading her to be deeply involved in her community. She was instrumental in developing Winnipeg Indigenous Rock the Vote (for the 2015 federal election) and, on January 31, 2016, she founded IKWE Safe Ride: Women Helping Women. Through her art Jackie expresses her ideas and opinions while striving to inspire dialogue on addressing her people's social issues.

"I can be inspired by ceremony and prayer, as well as kind and moving words. I love the culture of my people and this is where most of my inspiration comes from. Stories and art help us express complex ideas about who we are, what we value, and how we should behave. The teachings, values, and beliefs that shape our lives are passed down through oral tradition, religious teaching, literature, and art." Other art inspirations come from family anecdotes, dreams, and things from the media that help frame our experiences. Combined, traditional teachings, everyday landmarks, and life experience become symbolic signposts in the stories we tell about ourselves. To Jackie, painting is truly where her heart lies. Her happiest moments are when she is painting.

Jackie is known at the national and international level as an amazingly gifted artist. She was selected as one of eight Indigenous artists to represent Manitoba for the 2010 Olympic Games. In 2018, Jackie was Mik^w Chiyâm Teaching Artist-in-Residence, which operates in five secondary schools of the Cree School Board in Quebec.

IKWE is Jackie's second colouring book. Sacred Feminine, her first, was published in 2016. Jackie is dedicated to giving back to her people in as many capacities as possible.

Image editing & cover design: Melody Morrissette
Printed and bound in Canada

ISBN 9781773630731

Published in Canada by Roseway Publishing
an imprint of Fernwood Publishing
32 Oceanvista Lane, Black Point, Nova Scotia, B0J 1B0
and 748 Broadway Avenue, Winnipeg, Manitoba, R3G 0X3
www.fernwoodpublishing.ca/roseway

Fernwood Publishing Company Limited gratefully acknowledges the financial support of the Government of Canada through the Canada Book Fund, the Manitoba Department of Culture, Heritage and Tourism under the Manitoba Publishers Marketing Assistance Program and the Province of Manitoba, through the Book Publishing Tax Credit, for our publishing program. We are pleased to work in partnership with the Province of Nova Scotia to develop and promote our creative industries for the benefit of all Nova Scotians. We acknowledge the support of the Canada Council for the Arts, which last year invested $153 million to bring the arts to Canadians throughout the country.